Take a Look at Snakes

Written by Betsy Maestro

Illustrated by Giulio Maestro

Scholastic Inc.

New York Toronto London Auckland Sydney

No part of this publication may be reproduced in whole or in part,
or stored in a retrieval system, or transmitted in any form
or by any means, electronic, mechanical, photocopying, recording,
or otherwise, without written permission of the publisher.
For information regarding permission, write to Scholastic Inc.,
730 Broadway, New York, NY 10003.

ISBN 0-590-44936-2

Text copyright © 1992 by Betsy Maestro.
Illustrations copyright © 1992 by Giulio Maestro.
All rights reserved. Published by Scholastic Inc.
BLUE RIBBON is a registered trademark of Scholastic Inc.

12 11 10 9 8 7 6 5 4 3 2 1   7   2 3 4 5 6 7/9

Printed in the U.S.A.   09

Title page illustration: Garter Snakes

Since ancient times, people have had strong feelings about snakes — feelings of fear and disgust, or feelings of fascination and admiration. Long ago, snakes were thought to have power over life and death. Snakes were worshiped by many, including the ancient Egyptians and the Aztecs of Mexico.

Speckled Racer

Snakes were often used as symbols of good or evil in myths, legends, and biblical stories. People thought that snakes had magical powers that could bring them luck — good or bad. Of course this is not true. Snakes only seem mysterious because people do not understand them. Snakes are not really strange — they are just very different from most other animals, including humans.

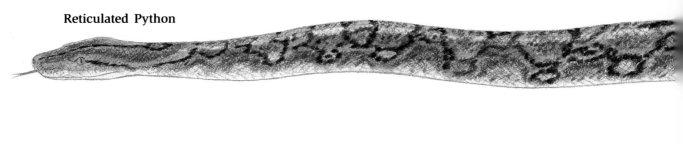

Reticulated Python

Green Anaconda

Most people do not see snakes very often. It may come as a surprise to learn that there are more than 2,700 kinds of snakes in the world. Some are over 30 feet long, while others may be only 4 inches. There are snakes that weigh well over 400 pounds, and tiny snakes that weigh less than one ounce.

King Cobra

Indigo Snake

Banded Krait

Coral Snake

Thread Snake

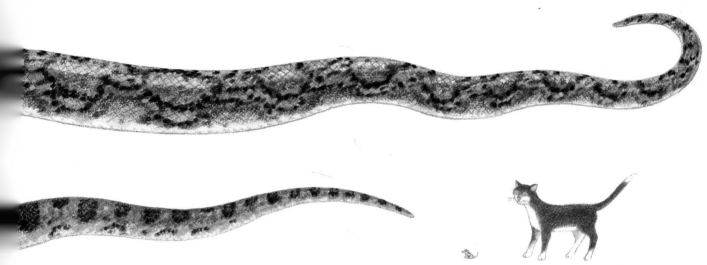

This is how big a mouse and a cat look next to these snakes.

Snakes live almost everywhere on earth, especially in places with hot and warm climates. There are very few snakes in cold places, and none at all in Iceland, Ireland, and New Zealand.

White areas on this map show where there are few or no snakes.

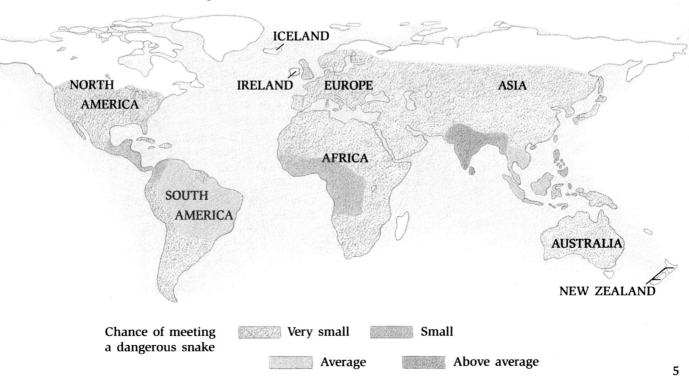

ICELAND

NORTH AMERICA

IRELAND

EUROPE

ASIA

AFRICA

SOUTH AMERICA

AUSTRALIA

NEW ZEALAND

Chance of meeting a dangerous snake

Very small

Small

Average

Above average

Emerald Tree Boa

Snakes live near the area where they hunt for food — in fields and forests, deserts and jungles, lakes and rivers. You can find snakes on the ground, in trees, in water, and even underground.

Black and Yellow Sea Snake

Many snakes have shelters called dens. The dens can be in hollow logs, under rocks, or in old animal burrows. Snakes sleep in their dens, and can hide there for protection from the weather and enemies.

Green Night Adder

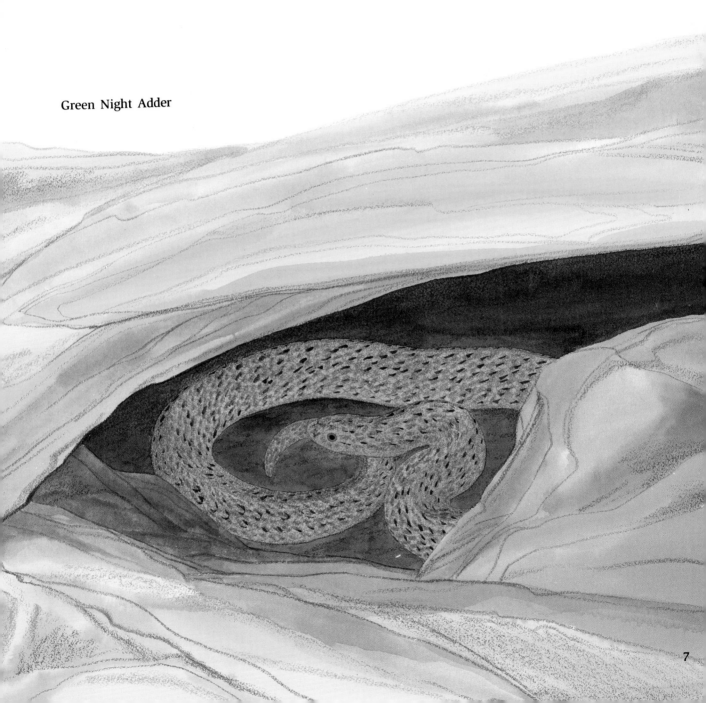

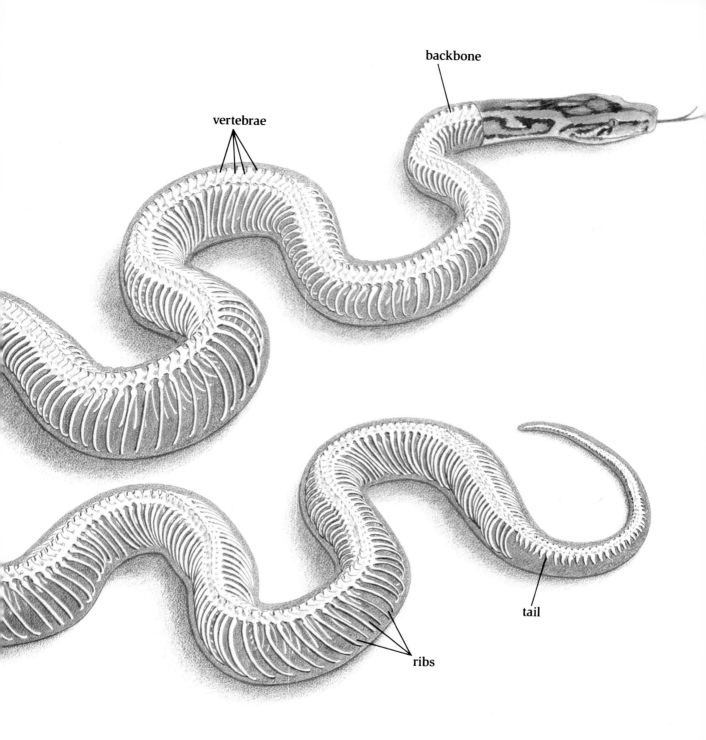

backbone

vertebrae

ribs

tail

A python's skeleton

8

A snake's body is long and very flexible. The snake can bend and curve its body in many places. In its backbone, there are as many as 400 to 500 small bones or vertebrae. The human backbone has only 32 or 33 vertebrae.

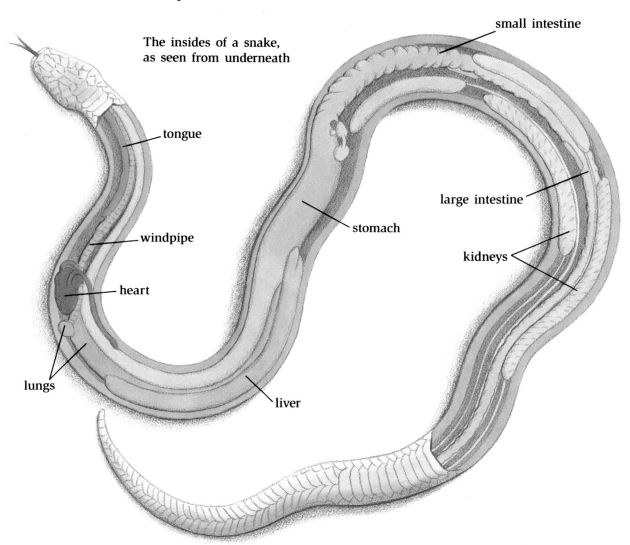

The insides of a snake, as seen from underneath

small intestine

tongue

large intestine

windpipe

stomach

kidneys

heart

lungs

liver

Snakes look like they are "all tail." Actually, only part of a snake's long body is its tail. Snakes have most of the same body parts inside that humans do. Since a snake's body is long and thin, its organs are long and thin, too.

The scales on a snake's back sometimes have raised ridges in the center of them, called **keels**.

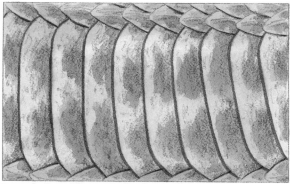

A snake's wide underbody scales are called **scutes**.

Snakes have unusual skin. The outer layer is made up of many overlapping scales of different sizes. People often think of a snake's skin as being wet or slimy. Actually, a snake's scaly skin is dry to touch. The colors and patterns of the snake's scales help the snake to blend in with the trees or ground. Snakes can be hard to spot.

Eyelash Viper

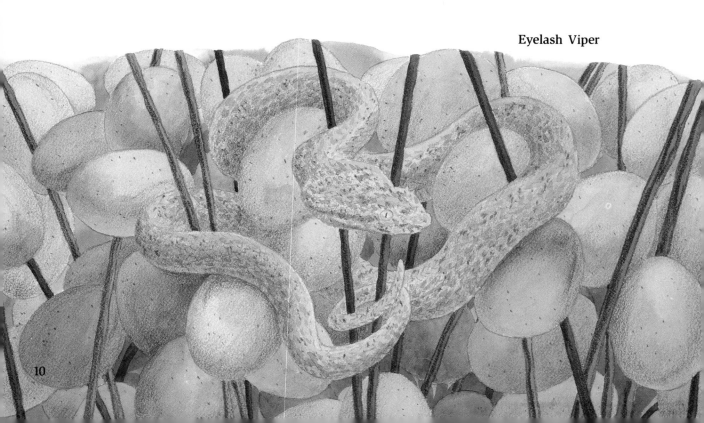

A snake's skin is very tough. Its scales protect the snake from injury, and help the snake to move. Snakes can move quickly, even though they do not have legs. Their broad belly scales grip the ground. Snakes also have powerful muscles under their skin. With the help of these muscles and scales, snakes can climb trees, cross desert sand, and swim through water.

Snakes can move in different ways, by:

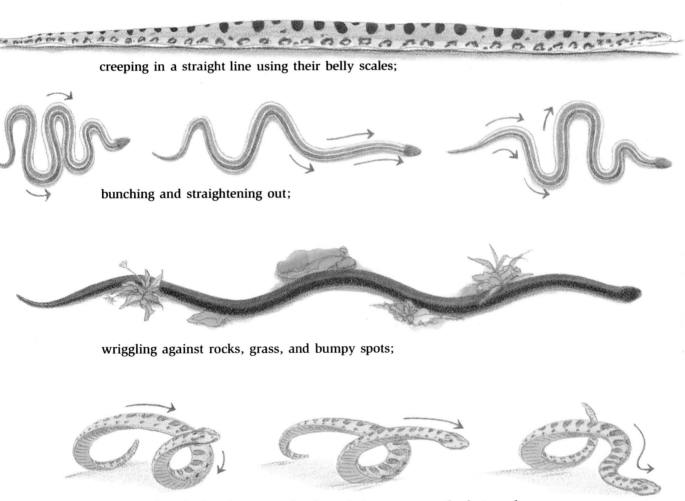

creeping in a straight line using their belly scales;

bunching and straightening out;

wriggling against rocks, grass, and bumpy spots;

looping their bodies. Desert snakes loop their way across the hot sand.

When a snake grows, its skin does not grow along with it. Every time a snake grows, it sheds its old skin and grows a new skin that fits its larger body.

The Rainbow Boa turns bluish-white before shedding its skin.

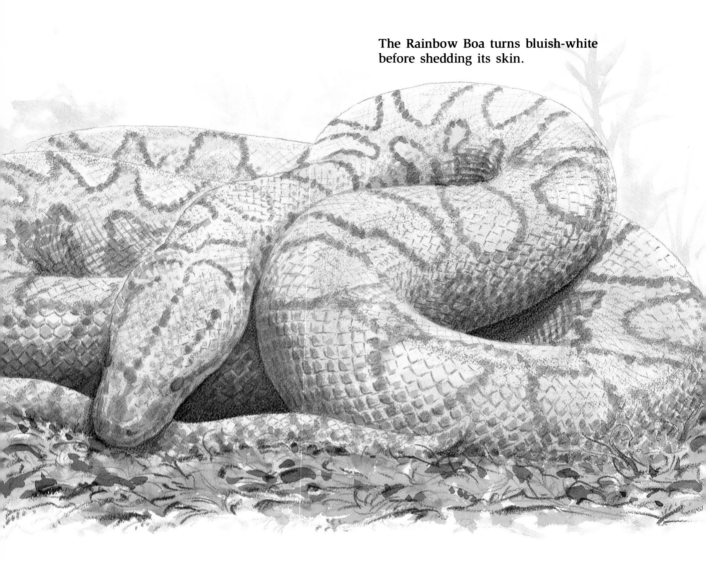

Because young snakes grow so quickly, they can shed their skins as often as seven times a year. Adult snakes usually shed their skins only a few times a year.

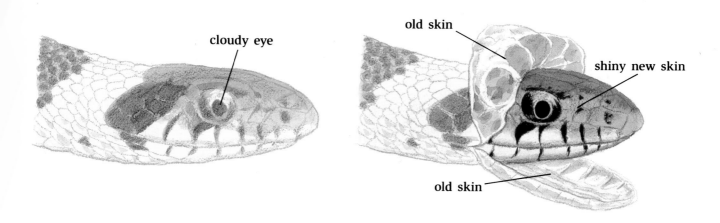

cloudy eye

old skin

shiny new skin

old skin

When a snake is about to shed its skin, the snake stops eating. Its eyes get cloudy, and it cannot see. Sometimes, it hides for safety. As the snake moves around, the old skin slides off in one piece. The new skin is bright and shiny.

Asian Keeled Snake

If you look at a snake's head, you will not see any ears. Snakes only have an inner ear. They do not hear sounds the way humans do. Instead, they depend on feeling the vibrations in the ground from nearby movement.

Garter Snake

Many snakes, like this Smooth Green Snake, can look at things only with one eye at a time.

The Oriental Whip Snake can see things in front of it because of its special eyes, and the shape of its head.

Snakes cannot blink or close their eyes. A snake's eyes are always open because snakes do not have eyelids. Compared with most animals, including humans, snakes do not see very well. They have trouble seeing things that are far away. Snakes are good at spotting movement close up, but when something is very still, a snake may not notice it.

Some small Blind Snakes spend most of their time burrowing in the ground.

Tree Python

Although snakes do not see or hear very well, they have other, special ways of finding out about the world around them. The snake's most important sensory organ is its tongue. The forked tongue of a snake is soft and delicate. It is totally harmless, and cannot sting or hurt in any way.

Yellow Anaconda

A snake can stick out its tongue without even opening its mouth. The snake's tongue flicks in and out, picking up clues from the air and ground. From these clues, the snake learns many things about animals and objects nearby. Although snakes smell through their nostrils, they really "smell" with their tongues.

The tongue picks up tiny specks of matter from the air and ground. When the tongue touches two tiny slots in the roof of the mouth, the sensing cells located here give the snake information about its environment.

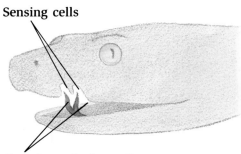

Sensing cells

Slots in roof of mouth

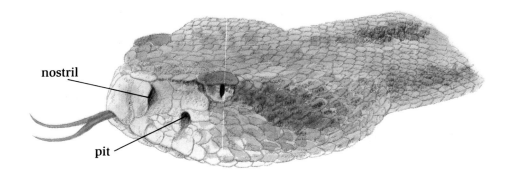

nostril

pit

Some snakes have another way to find out if other animals are nearby. Pit vipers, such as rattlesnakes, have deep pits or hollows on their faces. These pits are very sensitive to small changes in temperature. Because warm-blooded animals give off heat, pit vipers are able to locate their prey.

Rattlesnake

Finding prey is important because all snakes are meat-eaters. They must hunt for their food. Most snakes eat small animals, such as mice and rats, and birds and lizards. Snakes that live in or near water will eat frogs and fish. Very large snakes can kill and eat very large prey, such as deer. Some snakes are egg eaters, and some snakes only eat other snakes.

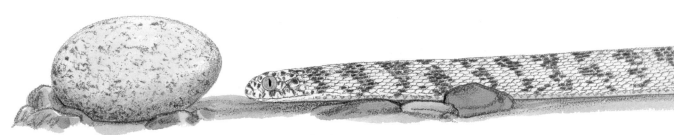

A snake can eat an egg that looks too large for it.

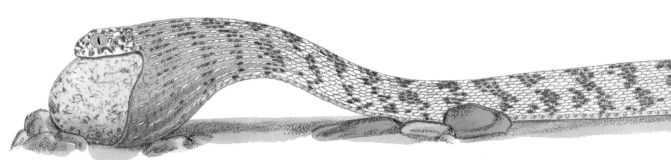

The snake's jaw and body can stretch to take in the egg without cracking it.

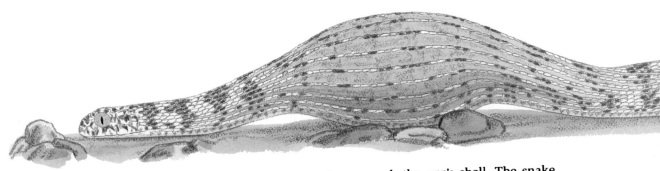

Special sharp toothlike spines inside the snake's throat crush the egg's shell. The snake swallows the soft inside parts of the egg, and then the broken shell is pushed back out.

Most snakes don't eat very often. After a big meal, a snake may not eat again for weeks. Some large pythons have gone for more than two years between meals.

A Ball Python digesting a big meal.

All snakes have teeth, but they do not chew their food. They swallow their prey whole. They can do this because their jaws are able to stretch open very wide.

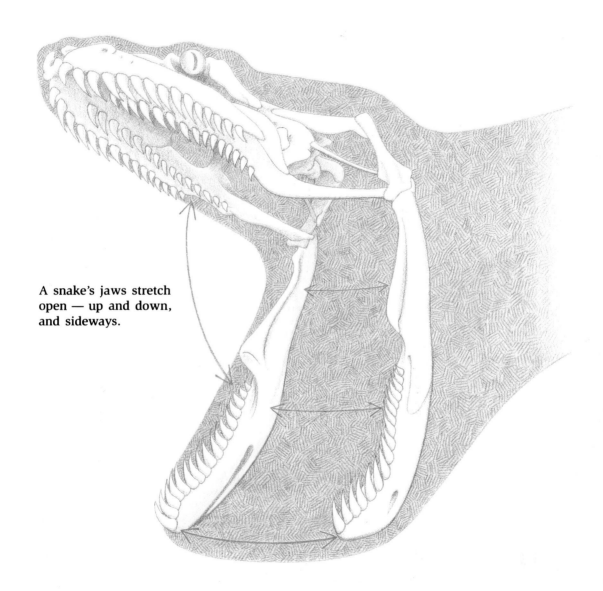

A snake's jaws stretch open — up and down, and sideways.

Since snake skin is so flexible, a snake can even swallow animals that are wider than the snake's own head.

Harmless snakes eat their prey live because they have no way to kill their catch before swallowing. They hold the prey with their teeth and body while they swallow. Since most of the world's snakes are harmless, this is how most snakes eat.

A Garter Snake catches a fish underwater and then brings it to the surface to swallow it.

A Viper stores its poison in two special sacs, one for each fang.

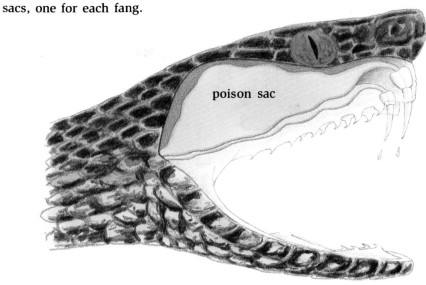

poison sac

Poisonous snakes kill their prey before swallowing them. Poisonous snakes have fangs — two long, curved teeth — that are hollow and needle-sharp. When the snake attacks, the poison or venom flows through the snake's fangs into the body of its prey. The snake waits for the poison to take effect before swallowing its catch. All snakes can be bitten or scratched while eating live prey.

A Viper's fang, larger than life-size. Poison can flow through each hollow fang.

There are about 400 kinds of poisonous snakes in the world. Fewer than 50 of these are truly dangerous to humans. Some poisonous snakes are too small to pose a threat to people. Other snakes have poison that may be too weak to harm humans. Sea snakes, cobras, vipers, and pit vipers are some kinds of poisonous snakes.

Sea Snake

The largest venomous snake is the King Cobra, which can be 18 feet long. One of the smallest is the Western Coral Snake, which is about 18 inches long. One unusual poisonous snake is the Spitting Cobra. It lives in Africa, and can hit the eyes of an enemy with a spray of poison from eight feet away.

Spitting Cobra

Constrictors also kill their prey before swallowing them. They do not have poison. Instead, they squeeze the prey to death by holding it with their teeth and wrapping their powerful bodies or coils around it. Within minutes, the captured animal dies because it cannot breathe. Constrictors then swallow their meal.

Some constrictors are giant-sized. The Reticulated Python of Asia is the longest snake in the world. One was reported to be 33 feet long! Anacondas are the heaviest snakes, and can weigh over 400 pounds. These huge snakes have no natural enemies except for people.

A South American Anaconda
constricting a Caiman

Snakes are cold-blooded like all reptiles. Their body temperature changes with the weather. When it is hot outside, a snake gets hot. When it is cold, a snake gets cold. If a snake gets too hot or too cold, it can die. Snakes must protect themselves from the weather. On cool days, they seek sunny spots. On hot days, they may hide in their dens and come out only at night.

A Coral Snake sunning itself

In places where winters are really cold, snakes hibernate and go into a very deep sleep. The snakes find a well-protected place where they will not freeze — such as a cave or underground burrow. They do not eat or move at all during hibernation. Although snakes usually live alone, they sometimes gather in groups to hibernate. By huddling together, they are able to stay warmer. In the spring, the snakes become active again.

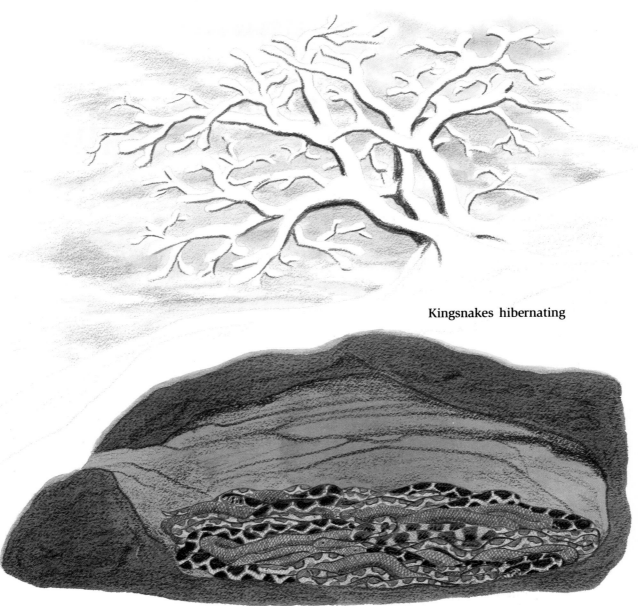

Kingsnakes hibernating

Rainbow Boas have live babies.

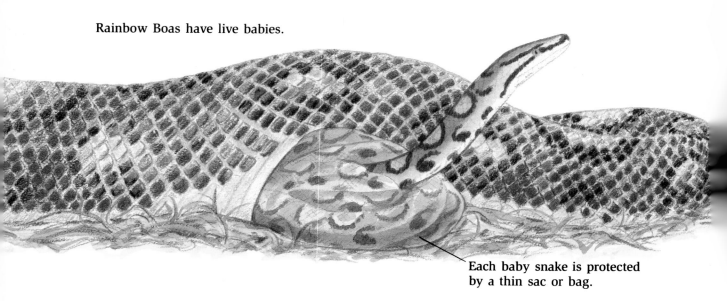

Each baby snake is protected by a thin sac or bag.

Spring is the time for mating. Male snakes seek out female snakes to mate. The baby snakes will not be born until many weeks later. Most female snakes lay eggs — from 2 to 100 eggs at a time. Some female snakes give birth to live young — as many as 80 babies at one time.

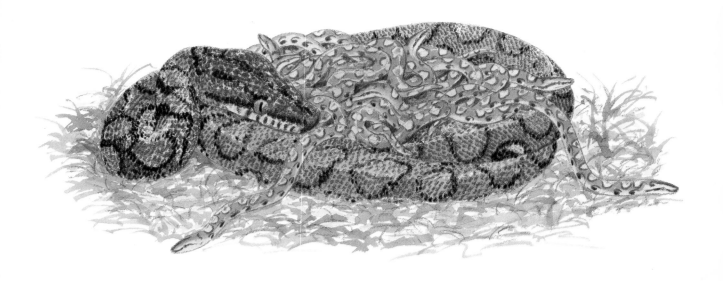

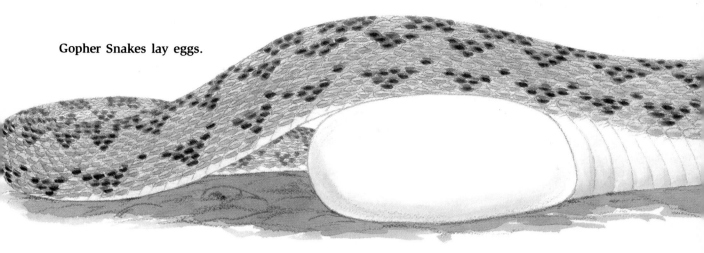

Gopher Snakes lay eggs.

Most female snakes leave as soon as the eggs are laid. They do not guard or care for the eggs. When the baby snakes hatch, they are on their own. Although they are born knowing how to hunt and defend themselves, many baby snakes will be eaten by other animals.

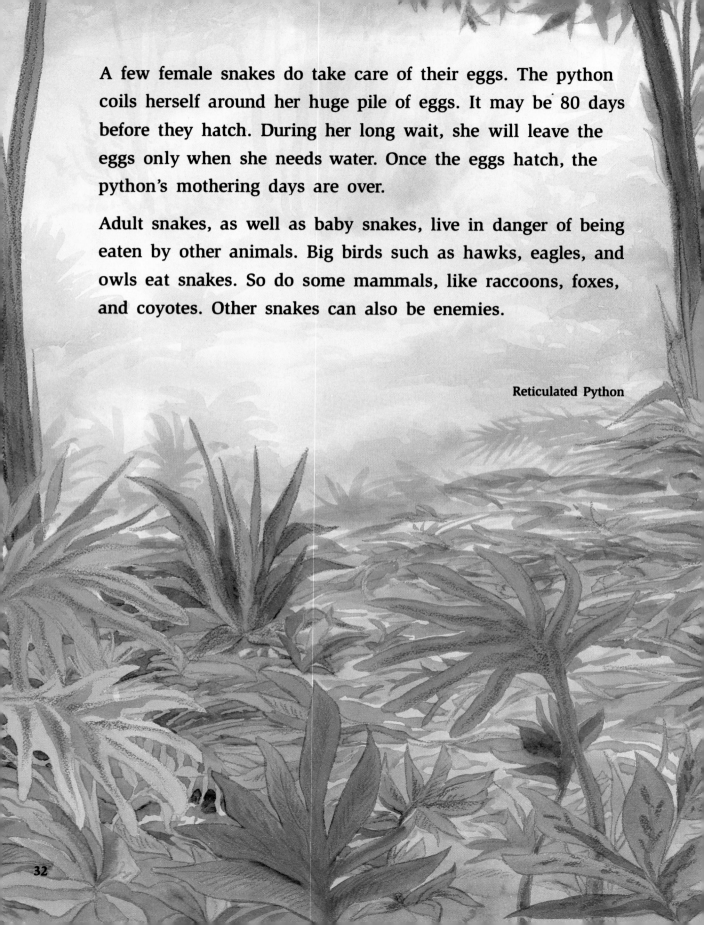

A few female snakes do take care of their eggs. The python coils herself around her huge pile of eggs. It may be 80 days before they hatch. During her long wait, she will leave the eggs only when she needs water. Once the eggs hatch, the python's mothering days are over.

Adult snakes, as well as baby snakes, live in danger of being eaten by other animals. Big birds such as hawks, eagles, and owls eat snakes. So do some mammals, like raccoons, foxes, and coyotes. Other snakes can also be enemies.

Reticulated Python

In order to survive, snakes must be able to defend themselves. When faced with an approaching enemy, most snakes will try to get away or hide. If snakes are trapped, they will try to fool their enemies by looking dangerous. Even harmless snakes can look frightening. They can make loud, hissing sounds, puff themselves up, and give off bad smells. Most snakes will only attack when they can't escape, hide, or scare away their enemies.

A Ringneck Snake startles its enemies by showing its brightly colored underbody.

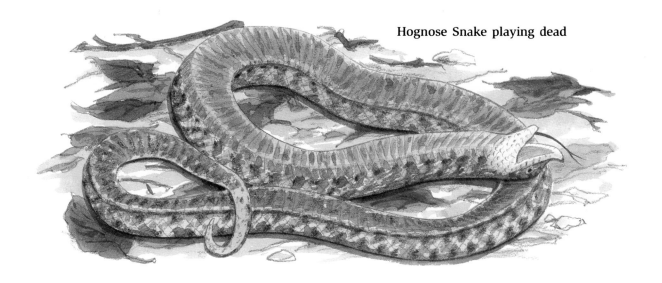

Hognose Snake playing dead

Harmless snakes often try to bluff their way out of trouble. The Hognose Snake first tries to frighten away the intruder. If this fails, the Hognose falls down and pretends to be ill. Then it flops over on its back and plays dead. Little Ball Pythons and Rubber Boas curl themselves into tight balls when they sense danger. Their heads are well-protected by their bodies. If the enemy attacks and they are lucky, only their tails will be bitten.

Ball Python

Rubber Boa

Even with all their defenses, few snakes live to old age. Of all the snake's enemies, the greatest threat comes from people. Because of their fear and hatred of snakes, people kill thousands of snakes every year. Many snakes are mistakenly thought to be poisonous or dangerous. It is important to remember that most snakes are harmless to humans.

A mother Racer with her babies

Because so many people live on the earth, more and more land is used for houses and other buildings. As land is cleared, many snakes and other animals lose their homes. As their natural living areas, or habitats, disappear, the number of snakes in the world grows smaller and smaller. Some kinds of snakes are already in danger of becoming extinct.

Actually, snakes help humans far more than they harm them. Snakes eat many animals that we consider pests, like mice and rats. This is a way of keeping nature's balance. Learning more about snakes makes it easier to look at them without fear. Then snakes can truly be admired for their beautiful colors and striking patterns, and for their unique way of life.

A Corn Snake looking for mice

DID YOU KNOW THAT . . . ???

A snake expert is called a herpetologist (her peh TOL a jist).

Baby snakes have a special egg tooth to help them break out of the egg. After hatching, the egg tooth drops off.

All snakes can swim. Sea snakes, however, can also stay underwater for up to five hours before coming up for air.

Snakes can digest almost every part of an animal, including its teeth and bones. Only hair and feathers remain undigested.

Snakes have a transparent lens, called a spectacle, covering each eye.

The King Cobra eats mostly other snakes. Its Latin name is *ophiophagus* (oh fee AH fa gus), which means snake-eater.

Ophidiophobia (oh FID ee oh PHO bee uh) is the word that means fear of snakes.

A baby snake can be as much as seven times longer than the egg it hatches from. Snake eggs have soft, leathery shells.

The African Black Mamba is the fastest of all snakes. It can move at about eight miles an hour.

Rattlesnakes only vibrate their tails when they are trying to protect themselves. It is a warning to enemies to stay away.

"Flying" snakes leap into the air from branches, and glide from one tree to another. They flatten their bodies to float on air.

Newly hatched baby snakes stay near their eggshells for a few days. They use the shells as a shelter, and they eat what is left of the yolk.

Scientists extract venom from poisonous snakes. It is used to make serum for treating snakebites and for other medicines.